For my daughter Giada and all little black girls with fierce attitudes around the world. Always remember, that attitude of yours can be used for good and help you run this world!

Little Miss Princess Attitude

written by
Jade Vaughn Simons

illustrated by
Tina Ochenante

Hi! My name is Giada, middle name being Armanda. Giada in Italian means Jade, which is my mommy's name (I'm her little mini me) and its been that way since the day I was made! Giada is the name or Gigi for short but you, you can call me... Little Miss Princess Attitude and please do not distort.

I AM TEENY IN SIZE BUT DON'T LET THAT FOOL YOU, MY PERSONALITY CAN GIVE YOU QUITE A SURPRISE!

My mommy and daddy have always called me their Little Princess Rainbow Unicorn and it's been that way since the day I was born.

Right now I don't have much hair up on top, but Nene & Grandma Nita say when it grows in everyones mouths will drop!

My poppy is my guy, the sight of him lights me right up, I swear I'm his little star in the sky!

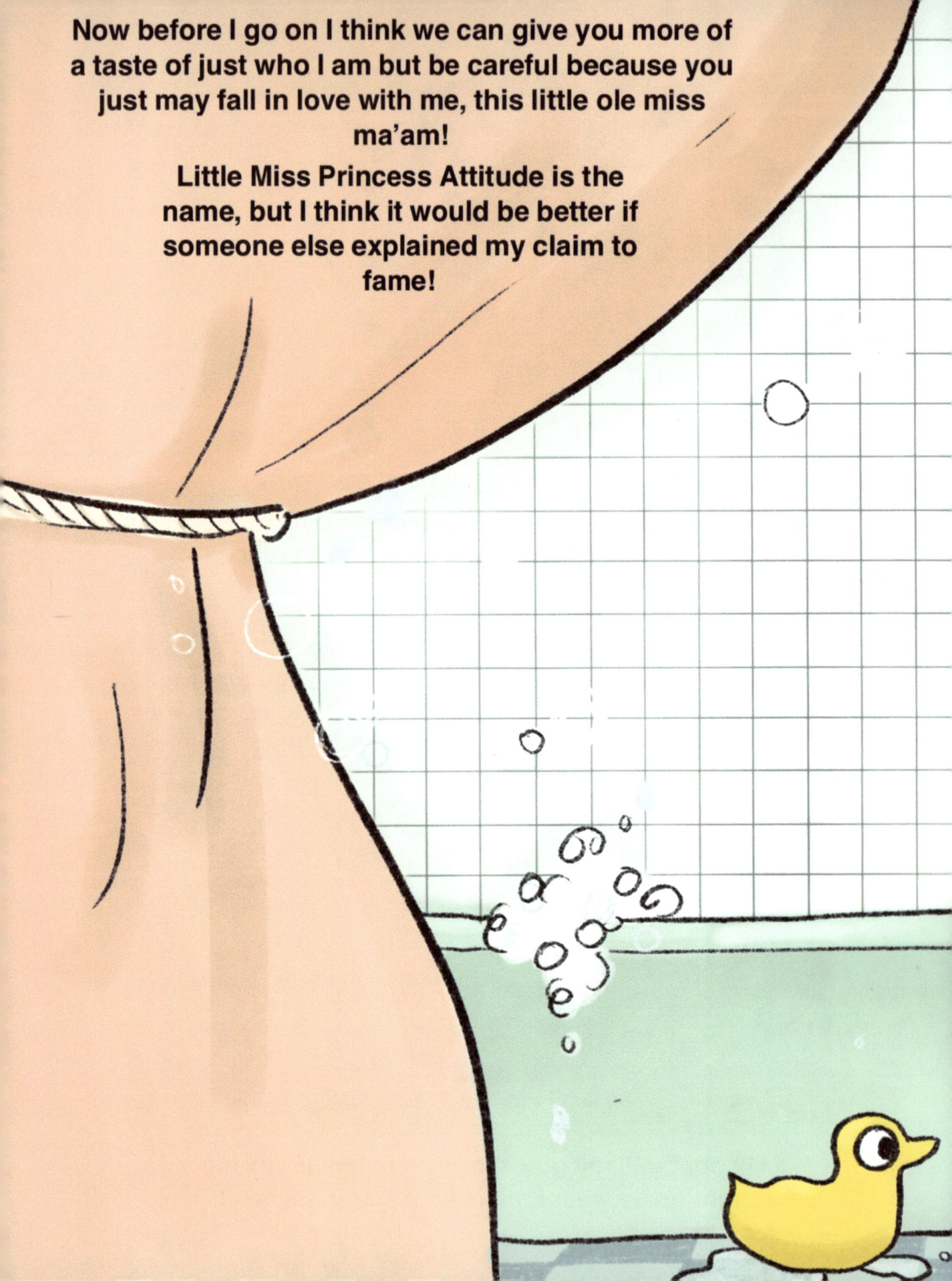

Now before I go on I think we can give you more of a taste of just who I am but be careful because you just may fall in love with me, this little ole miss ma'am!

Little Miss Princess Attitude is the name, but I think it would be better if someone else explained my claim to fame!

Little Miss Princess Attitude has facial expressions like no other and you may even get them twisted and think oh boy, she's rude my brother!

She walks into every room owning it as if she bought the place, so you better make room because she is going to need the space!

If a mirror is anywhere near you better know she is bound to stop and stare! A little kiss here and a little kiss there, she is in her own little love affair!

And when she hears a tune, she dances and moves like she is on top of the moon.

One of her favorite words is EWW, but that's definitely nothing new! If its yucky she is surely letting you know but try not to take it as a low blow!
Give her something yummy to put in that tummy and she'll be doing her little dancing jig, it's so cute you really may just flip your wig!

She moves her little hips and shoulders from left to right, her energy is truly a delight.
With the turn of her head and a little side eye, you won't know whether to laugh or cry but I promise she is as sweet as pie.

Mommy is her bestie and daddy is her first love, she has those two wrapped around her finger, constantly going beyond and above.

Little Miss Princess Attitude has not one, not two but three older brothers and when it comes to her they instantly become what you can call the bone-crushers.

Her Irish twin sister/cousin Alaya is always by her side, with these two together you can bet they're not letting anything slide.

Ohhh Little Miss Princess Attitude you sure do have magnitude. Now while this time I've spent telling them all about you has been fun, I think it's time to let you finish your story because you are our number one!

Hey hey! It's me again and it's time to bring this little story all about me to an end

You know, My Mommy always says to me I love your attitude, it's robust because in a world like this it surely is a MUST! She tells me don't take no mess and always do your best, keep this in mind always and you will forever be blessed.

While My Daddy says your attitude is wild girl but you're going to need it in order to run this world! He says so swirl, twirl, dance and move and always remember there is no one else like YOU!

My brothers say to me girl you're as fun as play dates in the sun and as bossy as mommy but we sure do love being apart of your posse.

What I say is I am me and there is no other person I'd rather be! I love every bit of me from tip to toe, every part of my attitude the highs and lows. This little me... yup I will forever *GLOW,* letting my love and energy overflow and believe you me you're not going to want to miss any part of my SHOW!

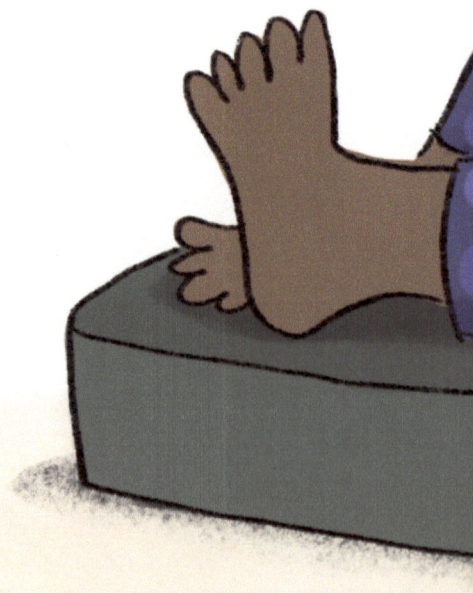

Welp that's the end... Well I mean that is until we meet again friend!

Jade has had a strong passion for working with young children since she was a young teen, which led to her earning her Bachelor's Degree in Early Childhood Education from Chatham University and her PA Teaching Certification PK-4. And I'm sure that same passion for children is also what led to her being a mother of three of her own little rascals who consistently keep her on her feet!

Growing up as a little black girl, outsiders would commonly assume she had an attitude due to her facial expressions and some of her mannerisms. So following the birth of her first and only daughter (her mini-me), who also gets the same commentary about her "attitude," it became vital for her to touch on how those "attitudes" do not have to be viewed as a bad thing. So she decided to team up with her close friend (Tina) who happens to be an amazing illustrator and creator, and bring this book to life, with hopes that other young black girls, families, and outsiders would get a new view on those little black girl attitudes that get such a bad rep!

Cheers to all the young black girls around the world. Keep being unapologetically who you are (attitudes and all)!

-Jade Vaughn Simons

Tina has been drawing and painting since she was a tiny tot. She made illustration her full time career in 2015 and graduated from Cambridge School of Art with a master's in fine art in 2022. She lives in San Francisco with her husband, son, and dog. If she's not painting in the basement while listening to an audiobook, you can find her at the beach or in a field.

www.ingramcontent.com/pod-product-compliance
Lightning Source LLC
Chambersburg PA
CBHW061402090426
42743CB00002B/114